I0160052

By Erik Lawrence
Copyright ©2014 Erik Lawrence

Erik Lawrence
www.vig-sec.com   erik@vig-sec.com

Printed and bound in the United States of America

First printing 2012
Second Printing 2014

ISBN 10: 1-941998-16-X
ISBN 13: 978-1-941998-16-8
EBOOK - ISBN 13: 978-1-941998-34-2
LCCN: Not Yet Assigned

ATTENTION US MILITARY UNITS, US GOVERNMENT AGENCIES, AND PROFESSIONAL ORGANIZATIONS: Quantity discounts are available on bulk purchases of this book. Special books or book excerpts can also be created to fit specific needs. For information, please contact:

Erik Lawrence
www.vig-sec.com   erik@vig-sec.com

Firearms are potentially dangerous and must be handled responsibly by individuals. The technical information presented in this manual on the use of the PA-63 pistol reflects the author's research, beliefs and experiences. The information in this book is presented for academic study only. Neither the author nor the publisher assumes any responsibility for the use or misuse of information contained in this book.

SAFETY NOTICE
Before starting an inspection, ensure the weapon is cleared. Do not manipulate the trigger until the weapon has been cleared of all ammunition. Inspect the chamber to ensure that it is empty and no ammunition is present. Keep the weapon oriented in a safe direction when loading and handling.

AMMUNITION NOTICE- this weapon fires the 9 x 18mm, not the 9 x 19mm NATO (9mm Luger.) Firing the incorrect ammunition will damage the weapon and possibly injure the operator.

Training should be received from knowledgeable and experienced operators on this particular weapons system. Vigilant Security Services, LLC provides this training and continually perfects their instruction with up-to-date information from actual use.

www.vig-sec.com

Table of Contents

Practical Guide to the Operational Use of the PA-63 Pistol, 9 x 18mm

Section 1

Introduction

The objective of this manual is to allow the reader to be able to competently use the PA-63 pistol. The manual will give the reader background/specifications of the weapon, instructions on its operation, disassembly and assembly; proper firing procedure; and malfunction/misfire procedures. Operator level maintenance will also be detailed to allow the reader to understand and become competent in the use and maintenance of the PA-63 pistol.

Description

The FEG PA-63 is a blowback operated, double action pistol with an aluminum frame and steel slide construction. The manual safety is located on the left side of the slide, and when engaged, safely brings the hammer down from the cocked position, and then locks the hammer, sear, and slide. The external hammer can be cocked manually for the accurate first shot in single-action mode, or can be cocked automatically by the longer and heavier trigger pull in double-action mode.

The Military standard PA-63 version sports a two-tone polished aluminum frame with black slide, grips, trigger and hammer assembly. While unusual for military issue in that a reflective polish was used, it was chosen due to its relative cheapness as well as quicker manufacturing time. Early problems related to the durability of the aluminum frame were resolved prior to the development of the PA-63 in 1961 with the production of the FEG R-61 Police Pistol. The addition of .1% titanium to the aluminum alloy solved premature alloy frame wear problems inherent in the earlier FEG aluminum framed pistols. This development was then applied to all aluminum framed FEG guns including the PA-63.

The PA-63 is fitted with fixed open sights as a standard.

Figure 1-1 FEG PA-63

The characteristics of the Hungarian PA-63 pistol:

A. Country of Origin: Hungary

B. Military Designation: PA-63

C. Cartridge Type: 9mm X 18mm Makarov cartridge

D. Type of Feed: 7 - round box magazine

E. Locking System: None

F. System of Operation: Blowback

G. Maximum Effective Range: 50 meters

H. Overall length: 17.5cm/6.9 inches

I. Weight unloaded: 595g/1.31 pounds

J. Weight loaded: 734g/1.62 pounds

K. Barrel length: 9.9cm/3.9 inches

Background

The FEG PA-63 (PA-63) is a semi-automatic pistol designed by and manufactured by FEGARMY Arms Factory in Hungary in the 1950s to replace their PP/PPK clone, the Model 48 which they had been manufacturing since the late 1940s. The PA-63 is a compact pistol, basically an FEG APK-9 chambered for the 9mm Makarov cartridge.

FEG stands for *Fegyver És Gépgyár*, which could be translated as "Arms and Machine Factory". It comes from the Hungarian "Fegyver- és Gépgyártó Részvénytársaság" ("Arms and Machine Manufacturing Company"). It is now known as the FÉGARMY Arms Factory (Hungarian: "FÉGARMY Fegyvergyártó Kft."). This company manufactured and exported a variety of semi-automatic pistols and rifles, including a copy of the famous Browning Hi-Power and the FEG PA-63, but currently only self-loading pistols (P9L, P9M, P9R, etc.) and break-barrel air rifles (LG 427, LG 527). In Hungary the company is also famous for its gas signal pistols, for example the GRP-9.

Operation

The PA-63 has a DA/SA or "Double Action/Single Action" operating system. After loading the pistol and charging the slide, one can carry the PA-63 with the hammer down and the safety engaged. To fire, the slide-mounted safety is pushed up to the "FIRE" position, after which the user pulls the trigger. The act of pulling the trigger for the first shot also cocks the hammer, an action which necessitates a long, heavy trigger pull. The firing of the round and cycling of the action precocks the hammer for subsequent shots, which are fired "Single Action" with a short, light trigger pull. After pushing the safety down to "SAFE," the hammer is safely decocked. Operation is semi-automatic, firing as fast as the user can pull the trigger.

The PA 63 pistol is a semiautomatic firearm working on the blowback principle.

Energy reaction generated by the fired cartridge charge thrusts the slide rearward against the recoil spring until it abuts against the receiver stop.

Rearward movement of the slide extracts and ejects the fired cartridge case, cocks the hammer and compresses the recoil spring. The stored energy of the compressed recoil spring then causes the slide to move forward towards the closed position, feeding the next cartridge from the magazine into the chamber.

The pistol is now cocked and loaded, requiring only a pull of the trigger to fire the next cartridge and each successive cartridge until the magazine is empty. If the loaded weapon is not already cocked, the shot can be fired by way of the double-action trigger mechanism.

The automatic firing pin lock is engaged at all times, except when the trigger is pulled. This feature provides additional safety if the loaded weapon is dropped with the hammer cocked.

Under normal circumstances, a shot can only be discharged by intentionally pulling the trigger. When the safety is in the "SAFE" position, the firing pin is shielded against contact from the hammer.

The PA-63s standard magazine holds seven rounds. When the last round in the magazine is fired, the slide locks open. However, the PA-63 has a Walther-like drawback. When the last round is fired, the slide is held back by the follower in the magazine. There is no slide lock; the magazine must be removed to lower the slide.

After feeding a new magazine, the shooter must actuate the slide by grasping the grooved surfaces at the rear of the slide with the non firing hand and pull the slide fully to the rear and release. Allow for full rearward travel of the slide prior to releasing the slide to chamber a round from the magazine. This action chambers a fresh round, and the pistol is ready for action again. When engaged, the PA-63's safety does not prevent the slide from cycling. The PA-63's magazine catch is, like the PP/PPK models, on the left side of the frame in front of the left grip panel.

Variants

The PA-63 was only manufactured in Hungary during the Cold War and afterwards. Below are variations that are sometimes confused for PA-63s.

FEG AP9 and FEG APK9 (compact)

Figure 1-2 FEG APK9 pistol

Caliber: .32 ACP and .380 Automatic which is sometimes also called 9mm Browning Short, 9mm Short, 9mmKurz, 9mm Corto, 9mm Kratak, 9x17mm and .380 ACP

Type: Double Action

Magazine Capacity:
AP9- .32 ACP is 8 rounds and AP9- .380 ACP is 7
APK9- .32 ACP is 8 rounds and APK9- .380 ACP is 7

Weight unloaded:
AP9- 770g/1.7 pounds
APK9- 730g/1.6 pounds

Overall length:
AP9- 17.9cm/7 inches
APK9- 16.5cm/6.5 inches

Barrel length:
  AP9- 10cm/3.9 inches
  APK9- 8.6cm/3.4 inches

Capacity: 7 rounds

This pistol was originally called the Model 48, but this name was later given to the Hungarian version of the Tokarev. The AP-9 is the larger model; a smaller version was also made, the APK-9. It was then called the Walam, and intended for sale to the Egyptians, but no such sales were made and this name was also dropped. The AP-9 was introduced in 1951, and was sold largely to Eastern European civilians except for some minor sales to the Hungarian Police. The action is quite similar to the Walther PP and PPK, though the appearance is different, and the frame is normally aluminum ally, with a steel slide.

Also called the FEG PMK-380

Figure 1-3 FEG PMK-380 pistol

Caliber: .380 Automatic, also called 9mm Browning Short, 9mm Short, 9mmKurz, 9mm Corto, 9mm Kratak, 9x17mm and .380 ACP

Bersa 380

Figure 1-4a   **Figure 1-4b**
Bersa 380 Thunder Dual Tone and Nickel pistols

Caliber: .380 Automatic, also called 9mm Browning Short, 9mm Short, 9mmKurz, 9mm Corto, 9mm Kratak, 9x17mm and .380 ACP

Type: Double Action

Weight unloaded: 635g/1.4 pounds

Overall length: 16.6cm/6.6 inches

Barrel length: 8.9cm/3.5 inches

Capacity: 7 or 9 round magazines

Poland also developed their own handgun design that utilize 9x18mm round. Poland has developed the P-64. While similar in appearance to the PA-63, being chambered for the same round, and labeled by some US gun retailers as "PA-63," these designs are independent of the PA-63 and have more in common with the Walther PP.

P-64 Vanad

Figure 1-5a P-64 pistol, right side

Figure 1-5b P-64 pistol, left side

Figure 1-5c P-64 pistol, field stripped

Caliber: 9 x 18mm PA-63

Type: Double Action

Weight unloaded: 635g/1.4 pounds

Overall length: 155mm/6.1 inches

Barrel length: 85mm/3.35 inches

Capacity: 6 rounds

The P-64 pistol (official designation *9 mm pistolet wz. 1964*) was developed in Poland during the late 1950s and early 1960s as a compact and lightweight replacement for Tokarev TT pistols, manufactured in Poland under soviet license. Following the Soviet road, Poland replaced the powerful 7.62 x 25mm ammunition with less powerful, but still effective 9x18 PA-63 ammunition. The P-64 has been used by both Polish military and police and can still be found in holsters of some Polish police officers. In military service, it was superseded in the mid-1980s by the P-83 pistol. The P-64 was small and light enough for a pocket or a concealed carry sidearm, but it has too small a magazine and too heavy a trigger pull to be considered as a valuable service pistol. The severely felt recoil also did not help to establish popularity for this gun.

Section 2

Maintenance

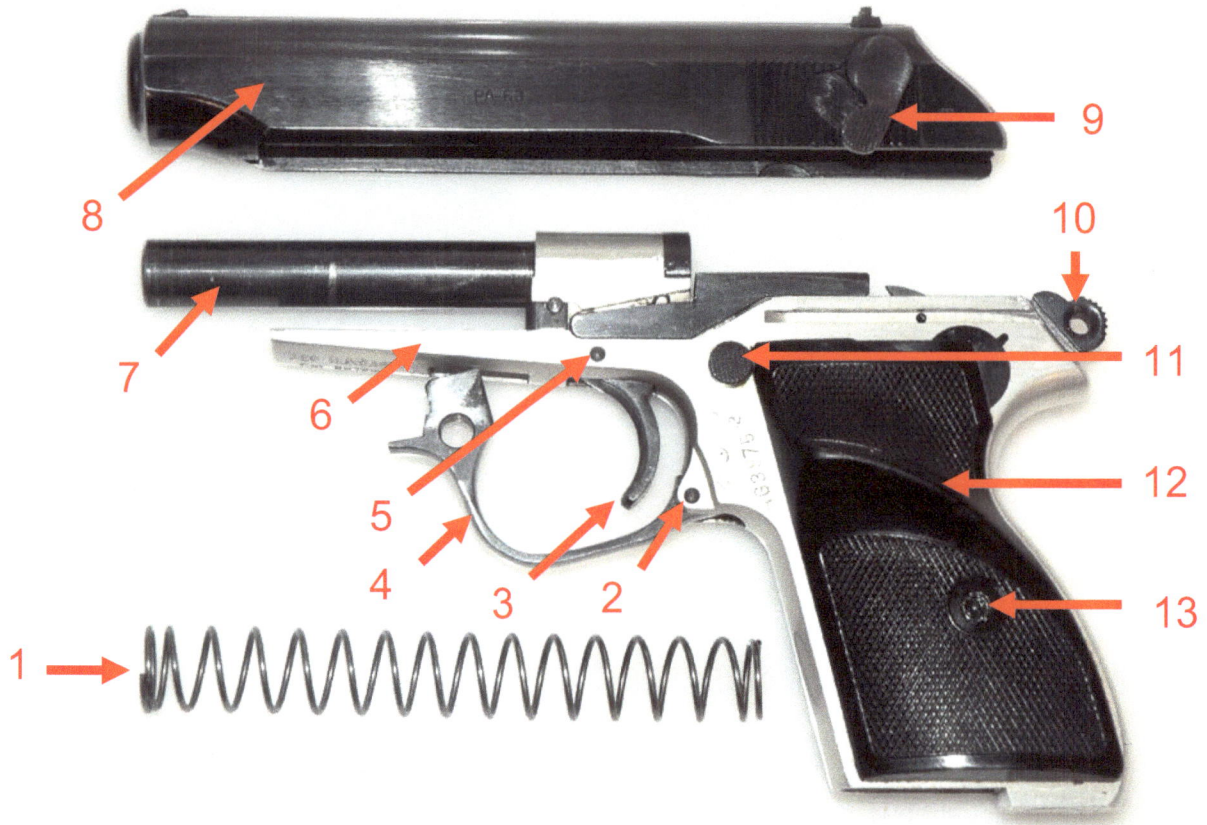

Figure 2-1 Parts of the PA-63 Pistol

1- Driving Spring	2- Trigger Guard Pin	3- Trigger
4- Trigger guard	5- Trigger Pin	6- Frame
7- Barrel	8- Slide	9- Safety Lever
10- Hammer	11- Magazine Release	12- Grip
13- Grip Screw		

Clearing the PA-63

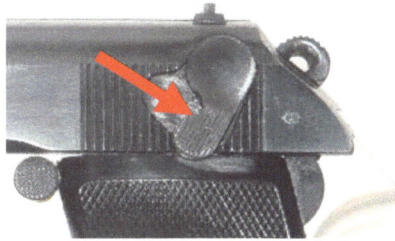

Figure 2-2 PA-63 Safety

A. Ensure the pistol is on safe and pointed in a safe direction (Figure 2-2).

Figure 2-3

B. Remove the magazine by pressing the magazine catch on the left side of the frame in front of the grip panel (Figure 2-3) and pull the magazine from the magazine well in the grip. You may have to pull on the front lip of the magazine to free it. Place the magazine in a pocket, magazine pouch or set it down.

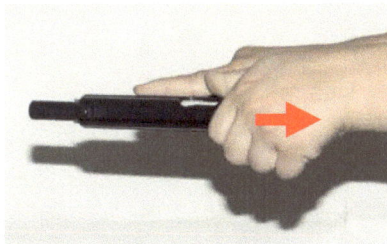

Figure 2-4

C. 1- Grip the serrations on the slide and 2- pull the slide rearward (Figure 2-4), allowing the round to extract and eject from the pistol and hold the slide to the rear. Observe the round extracting and ejecting from the ejection port; do not attempt to retain the round.

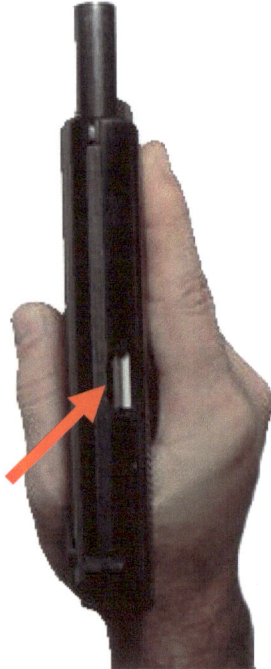

Figure 2-5a

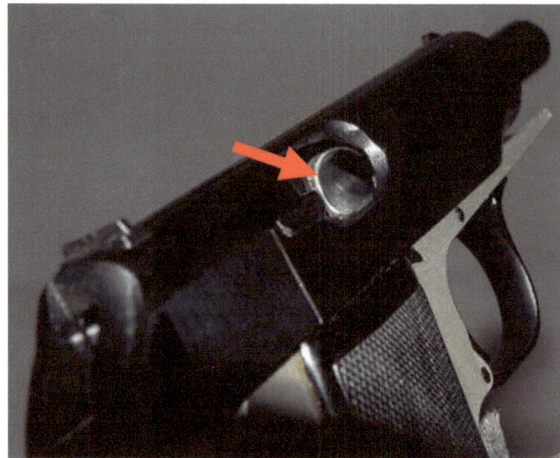

Figure 2-5b

D. Visually and physically check the chamber for rounds (Figures 2-5a and 2-5b). Once you have ensured the pistol has no magazine in it and the chamber is free of rounds, you now can close the slide by releasing pulling the slide riding the slide forward so as not to forcefully shut on an empty chamber.

Disassembling the PA-63 pistol

NOTE- Place the pistol's parts on a flat, clean surface with the muzzle oriented in a safe direction.

When the operator begins to disassemble the pistol, it should be done in the following order:

A. Clear the pistol and leave the magazine out and safety on.

B. To remove the slide,

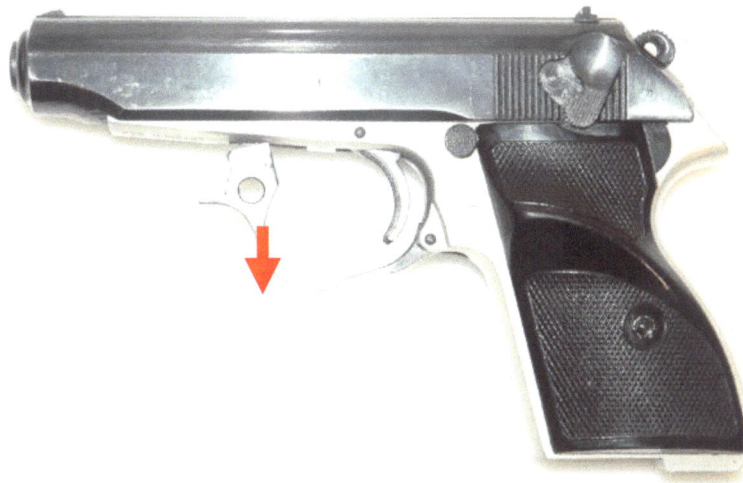

Figure 2-6

1.   While holding the pistol in your right hand pull the front of the trigger guard down with your left hand.

2.   Press the trigger guard to one side when the trigger guard will clear the receiver, slight movement, do not bend (Figure 2-6).

3.   Rest the trigger guard against the frame by its spring tension.

C. Remove the slide and driving spring.

1.   While still holding the pistol in your right hand, grasp the slide by its milled grooves with your left hand.

2.   Pull the slide fully to the rear of the pistol.

Figure 2-7

3. Lift the rear of the slide up and off of the frame and allow the slide be drawn forward by the driving spring until removed (Figure 2-7).

Figure 2-8

4. Once the slide is clear of the rear of the frame, ease the slide forward over the barrel (Figure 2-8).

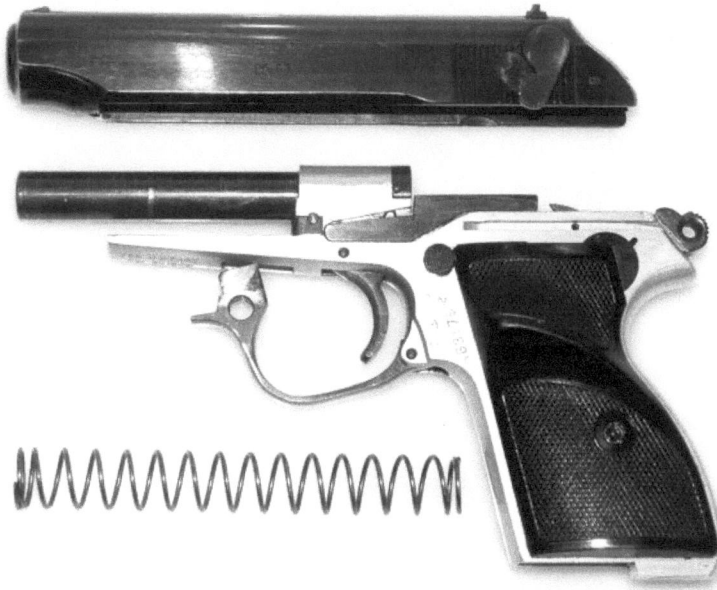

Figure 2-9

5. Pull the driving spring off of the barrel (Figure 2-9).

6. Further disassembly should be accomplished by qualified armorers or gunsmiths.

Reassembling the PA-63 pistol

A. Insure the hammer is cocked, the safety is in the fire position, and the trigger guard is down.

B. Reassemble and replace the driving spring and slide.

Figure 2-10

1. Slide the driving spring, small end first, over the barrel Figure 2-10).

Figure 2-11

2. Insert the driving spring front end into the circular front section of the slide (Figure 2-11).

3. Slide the barrel through the hole in the front of the slide.

4. Pull the slide fully back.

5. Press the slide down into position on the frame.

6. The driving spring will drive the slide forward.

7. Center the trigger guard and rotate it back into the frame.

Performing a Function Check on the PA-63 Pistol

A. Rotate the safety downward to the SAFE position (the hammer will fall automatically, but the safety blocks the firing pin).

B. Press the trigger (the hammer should raise, but not fall).

C. Rotate the safety upward to the FIRE position.

D. Press the trigger (the hammer should rise and fall).

Section 3

Operation and Function

Loading the PA-63 Magazine

A. Ensure you have 9 x 18mm Makarov ammunition; this ammunition is easily confused with 9 x 19mm NATO (9mm Luger) and .380 Automatic. Inspect it for uniformity, cleanliness, and serviceability. Check all cartridges for undented primers and only use issued ammunition.

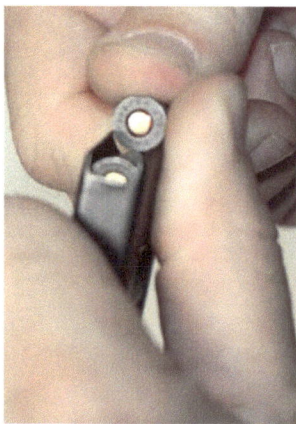 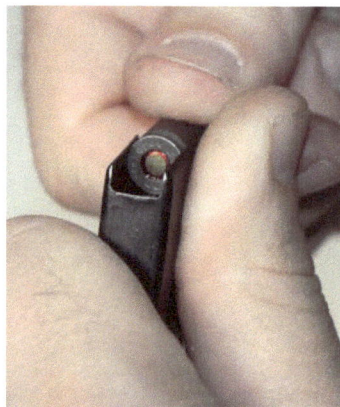 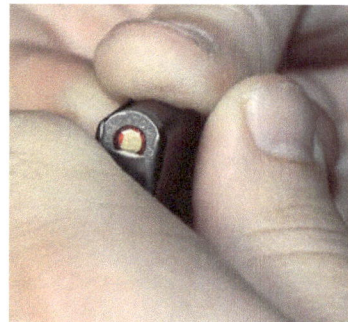

Figure 3-1b   **Figure 3-1b**   **Figure 3-1c**

B. Use your non-dominant hand to hold the magazine with the rounded front of the magazine towards your fingertips. Your non-dominant thumb is used as a guide so as not to let the cartridge roll off the follower or other cartridges (Figure 3-1a). With your dominant hand, one at a time, begin with the base of the cartridge at the front of the magazine follower and press the cartridge down and back to insert (Figures 3-1b and 3-1c).

C. The magazine can hold seven cartridges but due to overloading of the spring, do not carry the pistol in this configuration. Load seven and then load the chamber so you have six in the magazine and one in the chamber. Placing a cartridge in the chamber and releasing the slide stop can cause damage to the extractor, so load the chamber from the magazine only.

Loading the PA-63 Pistol

Figure 3-2

A. With the pistol pointed in a safe direction, place the pistol on SAFE (lower the safety lever) Figure 3-2.

B. Insert the loaded magazine into the magazine well. Fully seat the magazine with the heel of the hand to ensure it is locked in by the magazine catch.

C. Pull the slide by gripping the serrations on the rear of the slide, (not over the ejection port) to the rear and release allowing it to slam shut by its own spring tension. To ensure that a round has been chambered either removing the magazine to observe that only six rounds remain or perform a press check to observe the chambered casing through the ejection port. Ensure the slide is in battery (fully forward).

Firing the PA-63 Pistol

A. Orient downrange or towards the threat.

B. Press up on the safety lever to release the safety with a thumb.

C. As you orient your sights onto the target, press the trigger straight back so as not to interrupt the sight picture. As the PA-63 is double action, you will notice your first shot will have a heavier trigger pressure than subsequent shots that are single action (hammer already to the rear). The pistol may also be placed on fire and cock the hammer with your thumb to allow for single-action trigger pressure to fire.

D. When you have completed firing the pistol, place the safety lever into the SAFE (down) position.

Appendix A - Ammunition

9 x 18 mm Makarov is manufactured by many different countries and some can be rather old. Ensure you have 9 x 18mm Makarov ammunition; this ammunition is easily confused for 9 x 19mm NATO (9mm Luger) and .380 Automatic. Inspect it for uniformity, cleanliness, and serviceability. Check all for undented primers and only use issued ammunition. Many US manufacturers are making very high-quality 9 x 18 Makarov ammunition with modern bullets for self defense.

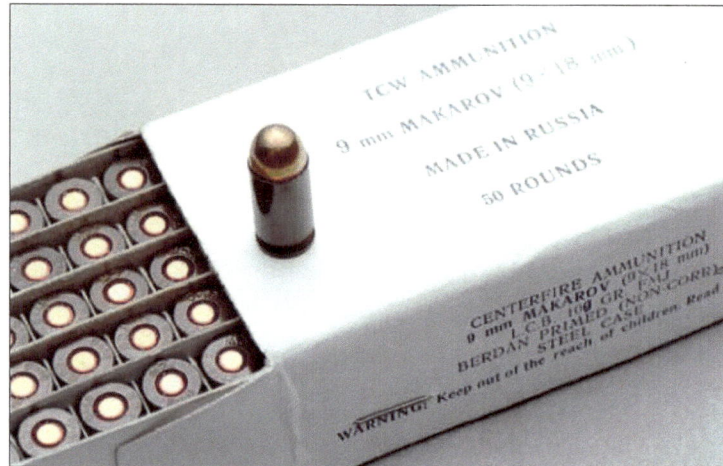

Figure B-1

Figure B-2 Russian 95 grain, FMJ, 1033 feet per second

Figure B-3 Hornady 95 grain, JHP, 1000 feet per second

Appendix B - Ammunition Comparison

9x18mm
Makarov

9x19mm
Luger

7.62x25mm
Tokarev

.45 ACP

PISTOLS AND SUBMACHINE GUNS

Size Comparison of
NATO vs. Non-Standard
Ammunition

5.56x
45mm

5.45x
39mm

5.56x
45mm

7.62x
39mm

7.62x
51mm

7.62x
54R mm

12.7x
99mm

12.7x
108mm

ASSAULT RIFLES

SNIPER RIFLES & MACHINE GUNS

Appendix C - Non-Standard Ammunition Packaging & Markings

Packaging

Russian small arms cartridges are packed in sealed sheet-metal containers, with two containers per wooden crate. Older Russian production used rectangular containers of heavy gauge galvanized iron with soldered seams. Around 1959, the introduction of painted, rolled edge, rounded corner, tin plate 'sardine can' containers became the standard.

Metal and wooden crates have standardized markings that identify the contents as to caliber, functional type, cartridge case material, quantity and cartridge/powder lot data. Specialized cartridges are further identified by a color code consisting of one or two color stripes which correspond to bullet tip color. AP cartridges with tungsten carbide cores are identified by two concentric circles instead of color stripes. Russian cartridge designation, packaging and marking practices are generally followed by former Soviet-Bloc countries; each, however, has introduced some modifications in designation and marking. Russian ammunition packaging can be distinguished from Bulgarian packaging, which also carries Cyrillic markings, primarily by the different factory codes. The factory code on the container also appears in the headstamp of the cartridges in the container.

Steel Ammo Tins
(Sardine Cans)

Wood Ammo Crate (Case)
(Contains 2 Tins + Opener)

Cartridge quantities and weights of wooden crates

Country	Manufacturer	Caliber	Rounds /Crate	Crate Weight
Czech Rep.	Sellier and Bellot	14.5 x 114	210	53 kg.
India	OFB	14.5 x 114	60	15.5 kg.
Russia	Unknown	14.5 x 114	80	23 kg.
Bulgaria	Arsenal	12.7 x 108	200	29 kg.
Bulgaria	Arsenal	12.7 x 108	200	32 kg.
Pakistan	POF	12.7 x 108	280	42 kg.
Russia	Unknown	12.7 x 108	190	29 kg.
Russia	Novosibirsk	12.7 x 108	160	25 kg.
Bulgaria	Arsenal	7.62 x 54(R)	880	25 kg.
Czech Rep.	Sellier and Bellot	7.62 x 54(R)	800	24 kg.
Russia	Novosibirsk	7.62 x 54(R)	880	26 kg.
Russia	Novosibirsk	7.62 x 54(R)	600	21 kg.
Russia	Unknown	7.62 x 54(R)	880	26 kg.
Serbia	Prvi Partizan	7.62 x 54(R)	1,200	39 kg.
Czech Rep.	Sellier and Bellot	7.62 x 39	1,200	28 kg.
Pakistan	POF	7.62 x 39	1,750	39 kg.
Russia	Barnaul	7.62 x 39	1,320	30 kg.
Serbia	Prvi Partizan	7.62 x 39	1,260	29 kg.
Sudan	STC	7.62 x 39	1,500	28.1 kg.
Ukraine	Lugansk	7.62 x 39	1,320	30 kg.
Yugoslavia	Igman Zavod	7.62 x 39	1,260	28 kg.
Yugoslavia	Igman Zavod	7.62 x 39	1,120	27.5 kg.
Russia	Unknown	5.45 x 39	2,160	29 kg.
Ukraine	Lugansk	5.45 x 39	2,160	29 kg.

Non-Standard Ammunition tin and crate marking - diagrams

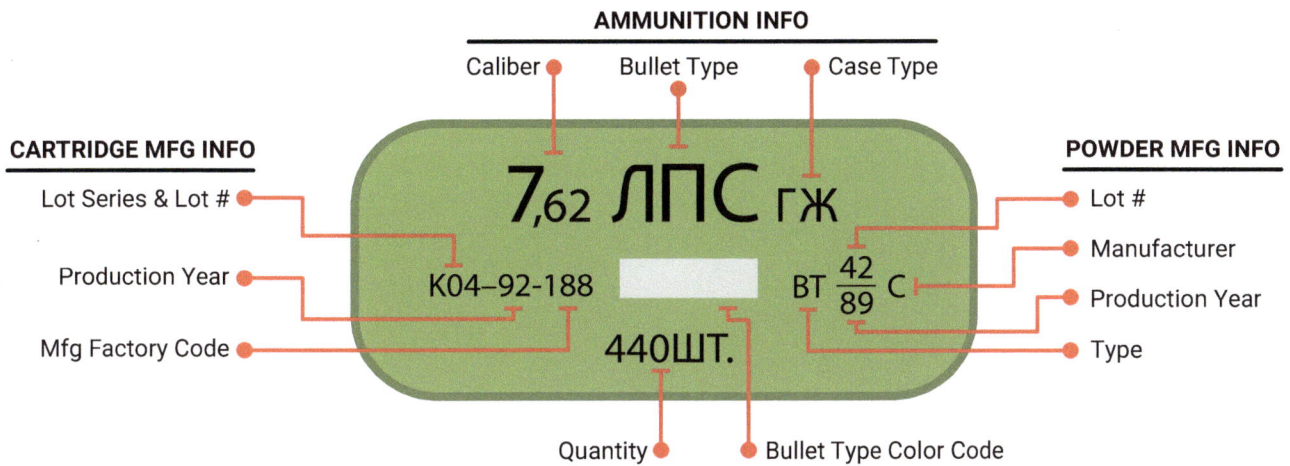

AMMUNITION INFO
- Caliber
- Bullet Type
- Case Type

CARTRIDGE MFG INFO
- Lot Series & Lot #
- Production Year
- Mfg Factory Code

POWDER MFG INFO
- Lot #
- Manufacturer
- Production Year
- Type

7,62 ЛПС ГЖ
K04–92–188
BT 42/89 C
440ШТ.

- Quantity
- Bullet Type Color Code

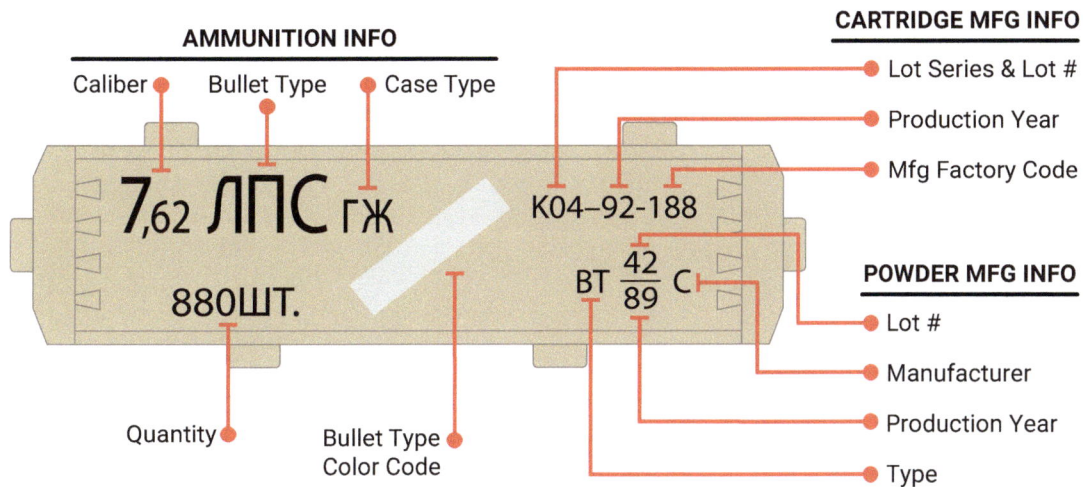

AMMUNITION INFO
- Caliber
- Bullet Type
- Case Type

CARTRIDGE MFG INFO
- Lot Series & Lot #
- Production Year
- Mfg Factory Code

POWDER MFG INFO
- Lot #
- Manufacturer
- Production Year
- Type

7,62 ЛПС ГЖ
K04–92–188
BT 42/89 C
880ШТ.

- Quantity
- Bullet Type Color Code

Non-Standard Ammunition tin and crate marking - Russian ammunition data

CASE TYPE MARKINGS

Mark	Meaning
ГЖ	Bimetallic case (gilding metal clad steel)
ГЛ	Brass case
ГС	Steel case

CARTRIDGE MFG FACTORY CODES

Code	Location
3	Ulyanovsk
17	Barnaul
38	Yuryuzan
60	Frunze (now Bishkek)
188	Novosibirsk
270	Voroshilovgrad (now Luhansk)
304	Lugansk
539	Tula
711	Klimovsk
T	Tula

Non-Standard Ammunition tin and crate marking - Russian ammunition data

BULLET TYPE MARKINGS

Mark	Meaning
Б Б-30 Б-32 БП	Armor-piercing
Б3	Armor-piercing incendiary
Б3Т Б3Т-44	Armor-piercing incendiary tracer
БС БС-40 БС-41	Armor-piercing with special core of tungsten carbide instead of carbon steel
БСТ	Armor-piercing with tungsten carbide core with added tracer
БТ	Armor-piercing tracer
Д	Heavy (long-range) with lead core instead of carbon steel
З ЗП	Incendiary
Л	Lightweight bullet
ЛПС	Light ball bullet with mild steel core
МДЗ	High explosive incendiary
П П-41	Spotting / ranging
ПЗ	Incendiary spotting / ranging
ПП	Enhanced penetration
ПС	Spotting / ranging with mild steel core
ПТ	Spotting / ranging tracer
СНБ	Armor-piercing sniper
Т Т-30 Т-45 Т-46	Tracer
57-У-322 57-У-323	Cartridge with higher powder charge
57-У-423	High-pressure cartridge
57-Х-322 57-Х-323 57-Х-340	Blank cartridge
57-НЕ-УЧ	Training cartridge
7Н1	Sniper bullet

BULLET TYPE COLOR CODES (Ammunition up to 14.5mm)

Color	Meaning
No color	Ball
White tip	Reference Ball
Silver tip	Light ball with steel core
Yellow tip	Heavy ball, or ball with torpedo base (on 7.62x54R)
Blue tip + white band	Short range ball 14.5x114 (only Hungarian and Czech)
Green tip + white band	Short range, tracer, (only Czech designation, only found on 7.62x39 with round nose)
Green tip	Tracer
Green tip & head-stamp or entire cartridge green	Subsonic ammunition for silencer-weapons
Red tip	Spotting charge, incendiary
Red tip + white band	Short range tracer ball 14.5x114 (only Hungarian designation)
Entire bullet red	High explosive bullet (7.62x54R after 1945)
Entire bullet red	High explosive bullet (on 12.7 and 14.5mm)
Magenta tip + red band	Armor piercing incendiary tracer
Black tip + red band	Armor piercing incendiary
Black tip + red shell	Armor piercing incendiary with tungsten carbide core
Black tip + yellow band	Armor piercing incendiary Phosphorus 12.7
Black tip	Armor piercing

** The bullet tip color codes in the table above will be the same color codes on the tins or crates, but they will be color stripes on the packaging.

Example:

CARTRIDGE
Black Tip + Red Band

TIN or CRATE
Black Stripe + Red Stripe

Appendix D - Non-Standard Weapon Identification Markings

General Identification Markings

There are various identification markings found on non-standard weapons. Typically the markings will provide some or all of the following information:
- factory name or stamp (proof mark)
- caliber & serial number
- selector lever markings/symbols
- rear sight mark/symbol

NOTE: Data tables are not all inclusive, but they cover the more common weapon manufacturers.

Selector Lever Markings on Kalashnikov Rifles

Upper/Safe Symbol	Mid/Full-Auto Symbol	Lower/Semi-Auto Symbol	Country
	Д	1	Albania
	L	D	Albania
	AB	ЕД	Bulgaria
	L	D	China
	进	单	China
	30	1	Czechoslovakia
	آلي	فردى	Egypt
	D	E	Egypt
	D	E	East Germany
	∞	1	Hungary
أ	ص	م	Iraq
	련	단	North Korea
	C	P	Poland
	Z	O	Poland
S	A	R	Romania
S	FA	FF	Romania
	1	3	Romania
	ЛР	ОГОНЬ	Russia
	АВ	ОД	Russia
U	R	J	Yugo/Serbia

Rear Sight Marks on Kalashnikov Rifles

Symbol	Country
D	Albania
П	Bulgaria
D	China
N	East Germany
A	Hungary
刀	North Korea
S	Poland
P	Romania
П	Russia
O	Yugo/Serbia

Non-Standard Weapon Identification Markings

Factory Stamps and Countries of Manufacture

The table of symbols below are factory stamps (proof marks) for non-standard weapons. The symbols will identify the country of manufacture of the weapon. *NOTE: This is not an all inclusive list, but it covers the more common weapon manufacturers.*

(10) Bulgaria	(21) Bulgaria	(25) Bulgaria	China
(386) China	36 China	66 China	China
Egypt	East Germany	(3) East Germany	(K3) East Germany
East Germany	(06) East Germany	Iraq	Iraq
North Korea	North Korea	(11) Poland	Romania
Russia	Russia	Russia	Russia
Russia	Russia	Russia	Russia

Yugoslavia/Serbia	Yugoslavia/Serbia	Yugoslavia/Serbia

M.70.AB2   ZASTAVA-KRAGUJEVAC

Appendix E - Non-standard weapons theory overview

There are three key concepts to understand when manipulating non-standard weapons. These simple and logical concepts are:

1. CYCLE OF OPERATIONS
2. OPERATING SYSTEMS
3. LOCKING SYSTEMS

Firearm design trends are shared across region, manufacturer and class of weapon and are relatively obvious to recognize.

Keep in mind that firearms are essentially simple machines that harness the energy created by the fired cartridge to operate the system.

CYCLE OF OPERATIONS (COO)

The cycle of operations is a crucial basis for understanding how the weapon operates and for function/malfunction diagnosis. Each specific malfunction will correspond to a specific step or sometimes two in the COO. A failure in the system at a certain point, will by default, cause a failure of omission of all subsequent steps. (example – a failure to properly extract will manifest as a failure to eject.)

The COO will vary based on the type of operating and locking systems. Once the operating and locking systems of the weapon are known, the COO is logical.

The examples below all start from a standard reference point: the weapon is loaded, charged, placed on fire and the trigger is pulled.

'Cycle of Operations' Examples:

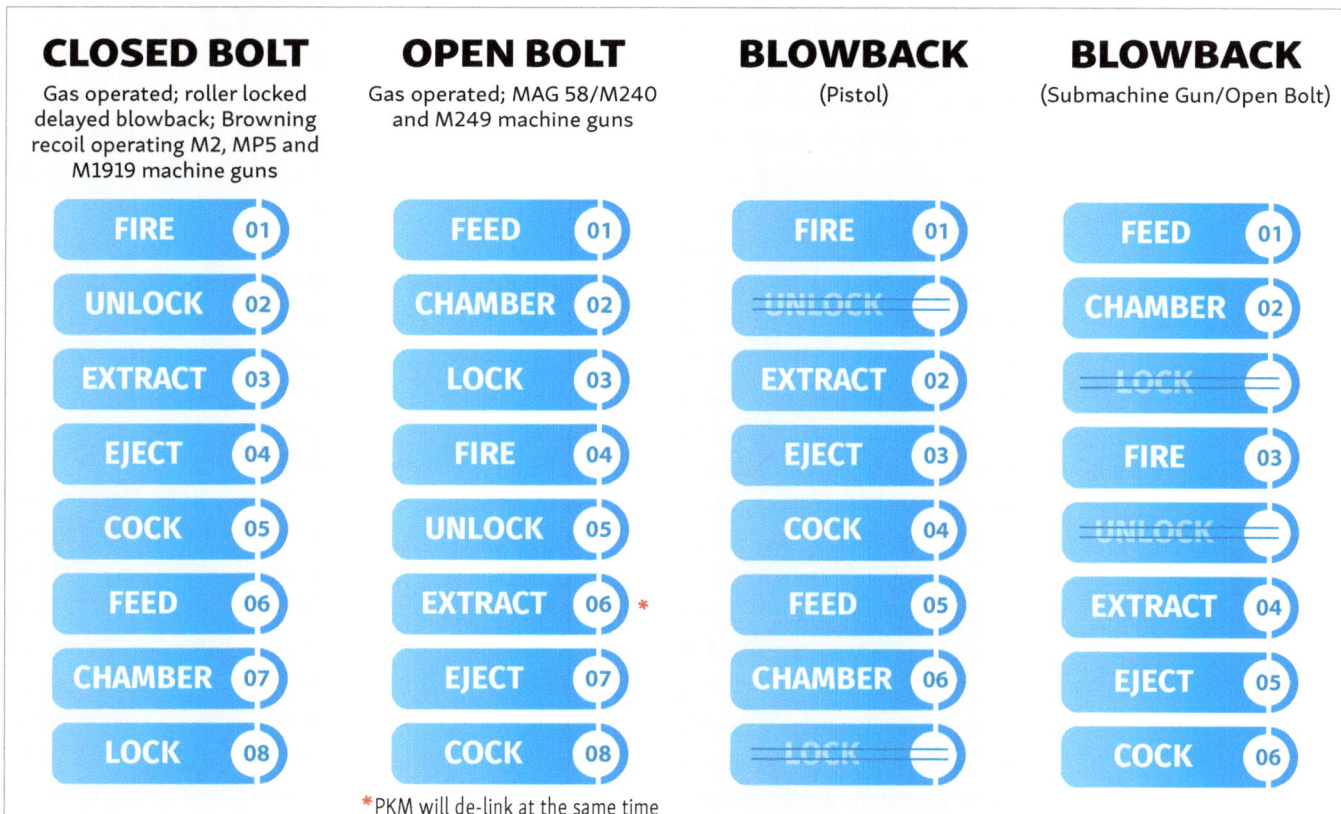

CLOSED BOLT	OPEN BOLT	BLOWBACK	BLOWBACK
Gas operated; roller locked delayed blowback; Browning recoil operating M2, MP5 and M1919 machine guns	Gas operated; MAG 58/M240 and M249 machine guns	(Pistol)	(Submachine Gun/Open Bolt)
FIRE 01	FEED 01	FIRE 01	FEED 01
UNLOCK 02	CHAMBER 02	~~UNLOCK~~	CHAMBER 02
EXTRACT 03	LOCK 03	EXTRACT 02	~~LOCK~~
EJECT 04	FIRE 04	EJECT 03	FIRE 03
COCK 05	UNLOCK 05	COCK 04	~~UNLOCK~~
FEED 06	EXTRACT 06 *	FEED 05	EXTRACT 04
CHAMBER 07	EJECT 07	CHAMBER 06	EJECT 05
LOCK 08	COCK 08	~~LOCK~~	COCK 06

*PKM will de-link at the same time

Non-standard weapons theory overview *(continued …)*

⚙ **OPERATING SYSTEMS**

1. **Direct Impingement**- a type of gas operation that directs gas from a fired cartridge directly to the bolt carrier or slide assembly to cycle the action. (AR-15/M4 variants)

2. **Long-stroke piston system**- the piston is mechanically fixed to the bolt group and moves through the entire operating cycle. (AK variants)

3. **Short-stroke piston system (tappet system)**- the piston moves separately from the bolt group. It may directly push the bolt group parts as n the M1 carbine or operate through a connecting rod. (HK 416, AR180, POF, LWRC, FN FAL)

4. **Blowback**- the system of operation for self-loading firearms that obtains energy from the motion of the cartridge case as it is pushed to the rear by expanding gases created by the ignition of the propellant charge. (STEN, Makarov, M3 Grease Gun)

5. **Short recoil action**- the barrel and slide recoil only a short distance before they unlock and separate. The barrel stops quickly, and the slide continues rearward compressing the recoil spring and performing extraction, ejection and finally feeding a fresh round from the magazine in the counter recoil phase. During the last portion of its forward travel, the slide locks into the barrel and pushes the barrel back into battery. *(This is found in most handguns chambered for 9x19mm Parabellum or greater caliber. Smaller calibers, 9x18mm Makarov and below, generally use the blowback method of operation due to lower chamber pressure and associated simplicity of design.)

6. **Roller-locked, delayed-blowback**- when the bolt is closed, the rollers carried in the bolt are wedged into the receiver recesses. On firing, the rollers must be forced out of the recesses at great mechanical disadvantage, delaying the opening of the bolt, even with full power 7.62mm NATO (.308 Winchester) rifle cartridges used in the G3/HK 91 (G3, HK 91, HK 93, HK 53, MP5 variants)

7. **Inertia operated systems**- the bolt body is separated from the locked bolt body to remain stationary while the recoiling gun and locked bolt head moves rearward. This movement compresses the spring between the bolt head and bolt body, storing the energy required to cycle the action. Benelli shotguns.

Non-standard weapons theory overview *(continued …)*

🔒 LOCKING SYSTEMS

1. **None** - all blowback pistols and some submachine guns – (STEN, UZI, M3 Grease Gun, Makarov, and CZ 82)

2. **Roller** - (HK variants, MG3, MG34, MG 42 and CZ 52)

3. **Rotating bolt** - (AK, Stoner, M60, and M249)

4. **Tilting bolt** - (SKS, FN FAL and MAG 58/M240)

5. **Tilting barrel** - (Tokarev TT33, Sig variants, M1911 variants and Glock variants)

6. **Rotating barrel** - (MAB P15, Colt All American 2000, and Beretta 8000)

7. **Locking flaps** - (RPD, DP/DPM and DShK)

8. **Falling locking block** - (P38, M9, and VZ58)

Function check
Checking the mechanical function of a weapon by replicating, without ammunition, the firing modes from the lowest rate of fire (SAFE if applicable) to the highest in a progressive sequence (not by selector location). The parts checked are the safety/safeties, sear and disconnector.

M4A1
1. Ensure the rifle is clear
2. Charge and place the weapon on SAFE
3. Attempt to fire (weapons should not FIRE, safety is functioning)
4. Place the weapon on SEMI, pull the trigger and hold it to the rear (hammer should fall, trigger/sear functioning)
5. Maintain the trigger to the rear and cycle the bolt
6. Release the trigger and listen for a metallic click (disconnector functioning)
7. Pull the trigger again and the hammer should fall
8. Charge the weapon and place on AUTO
9. Pull the trigger and hold it to the rear then cycle the bolt more than once
10. Release the trigger and pull it again, nothing should happen (auto sear is functioning)
11. Charge the weapon then pull the trigger again and the hammer should fall
12. Function check complete

Significant visual indicators
- Any checked, knurled or serrated surface
- Any movable lever or switch
- Pins with gripping surfaces
- Index marks (two lines that need to be aligned to disassembled (CZ 75)
- Recoil spring with ends of different diameters

www.ingramcontent.com/pod-product-compliance
Lightning Source LLC
Chambersburg PA
CBHW061058090426
42742CB00002B/88